101

SUCCESS TIPS
FOR KIDS

By Kids for Kids

Reese Haller and Parker Haller

Personal Power Press, Inc.
Merrill, Michigan

101
SUCCESS TIPS
FOR KIDS

By Kids for Kids

Copyright 2008 by Reese Haller, Parker Haller, and Personal Power Press

Library of Congress Catalogue Card Number: 2008937152

ISBN #: 978-0-9772321-9-2

Printed in the United States of America

Personal Power Press, Inc.
P.O. Box 547
Merrill, MI 48637

Cover Design
Zachary Parker/kadak graphics
zdp431@gmail.com

Book Design
Connie Thompson/Graphics Etcetera
connie2@lighthouse.net

TABLE OF CONTENTS

FOREWORD

By Sharon Travis

Success is something we all would like to have. How do we measure it? How do we attain it? Who can help us?

Two gifted youngsters, Reese and Parker Haller, took what they have learned in their young lives and compiled a list of 101 pointers to help children become successful. In this book these youngsters share their thoughts and ideas about the life lessons they have been taught.

The great news is, *101 Success Tips for Kids* is a tool not only for kids. Even adults can use it to reach their goals for success. I've already started to use some of these tips to help me in my own life. I can't wait to share this book with my second-grade students. Advice from one *"kid"* to another that has usable substance and personal meaning will go a long way in improving the lives of everyday children.

Reese and Parker Haller are both talented young authors from Bay City, Michigan. I've had the honor of having these boys as students in The Program for the Academically Talented in the Bay City public schools. As second- and third-graders, they both displayed an advanced ability to be very creative in their written expression. Our school district promotes using *The Six Traits of Writing* in our curriculum, and both Reese and Parker were particularly successful at incorporating the traits of word choice, voice and ideas in their writing samples. Using these traits requires the author to be creative and imaginative; characteristics these boys have no shortage of. In my classroom Parker and Reese approached writing with excitement and enthusiasm, often putting a great deal of thought into the pieces they were creating. Having seen their writing first hand, it is no surprise to me that they have written such an incredible book.

Although these boys are only eight and eleven years old, they are already successful. Reese is the author of the *Fred the Mouse*™ book series and Parker the author and illustrator of *Animal Facts: Mini-Books for the Early Reader.* Parker also produces a children's newsletter that has made its way into twenty-eight states.

Successful children are the result of successful parenting. Thomas and Valerie Haller provide a solid family foundation that is filled with learning opportunities and the encouragement that allows these children to flourish and continue to develop a skill they love: writing. As an educator, it has been exciting for me to watch these boys continue to write in the home setting for the pure joy of writing and not just to complete a classroom assignment.

I would like to personally thank Parker and Reese for giving such a fine example of setting and completing goals. Every time I read one of their books to my students it stirs excitement in them to become accomplished writers. Parker and Reese have proven to our youth that children can do great things. They have made my job easier! I can't wait to see what they come up with next!

Sharon Travis
Educator - 2nd Grade
The Program for the Academically Talented
Bay City Public Schools

INTRODUCTION

Welcome to our collection of tips, ideas and suggestions that we've learned from the important adults in our lives. What you hold in your hands is what we've heard and talked about with our Grandpa Barnes (we call him Bondy) and Grandma Barnes (we call her Grammy), our Grandma Jo, our Uncle Marty and Aunt Jen, our dad's best friend Lou (we call him Uncle Lou), our dad and, most importantly, our mom.

We remember these tips because our parents are always reminding us of them and telling us to use them. So we used them and we still do. Now we want to pass them on to you so you can use them too. Go ahead, be who you want to be now. Create the success you want.

THE PEOPLE WHO GAVE US THESE TIPS

The adults mentioned above are all very successful people. Bondy was the city manager of Bay City for over fifteen years. He is now retired and lives in Florida in the winter and Michigan in the summer. Grammy took care of us when we were babies until we went to school. She is very gentle and cares about people's feelings. Grandma Jo is our dad's mom. She lives in Wisconsin all by herself and she loves to play card games and be silly. Grandma Jo is pretty old but acts like a kid. She's taught us a lot about having fun in new and different ways. Uncle Marty is an ear, nose and throat doctor in Milwaukee. He loves to fish for salmon in Lake Michigan when he is not working at the office or in surgery. Aunt Jen keeps Uncle Marty's office running smoothly. She also keeps everything very clean. Our dad says you can eat off of Aunt Jen's kitchen floor if you want to. We think he says that just because she's his big sister, even though the floor is really clean. Uncle Lou is a psychology professor at Saginaw Valley State University. He teaches college students how to do research projects and stuff about the brain called neuropsychology. Our dad is a child and relationship therapist, an author of five books, and a radio personality. On the radio they call him "Dr. Tom, the Love Doctor." It's kind of embarrassing but Mom thinks it's cute.

We think our mom is the most successful one of all. She has been a kindergarten teacher in the public schools for twenty years. She loves kids, loves to read, especially to us, and is the happiest person we know. Even though we think she sings too much sometimes, we are most comfortable when we are with our mama.

A LITTLE ABOUT OUR SUCCESS

Okay, so we're only eleven and eight, but that doesn't mean we aren't successful. We are both published authors. Reese published his first book at age eight. He now has four books in the award-winning *Fred the Mouse*™ series. He has been a judge in a national writing contest for three years. He is also on an advisory panel and a spokesperson for a new national monument called the Statue of Responsibility. In addition, he is in his fourth year of traveling to schools all over the country presenting his eight secrets to successful writing in "Catching the Writing Bug: From One Kid to Another."

Parker published his first book at age seven, *Animal Facts: Mini-Books for the Early Reader.* He is also the illustrator of *Animal Facts.* It has 140 pencil drawings of animals. In the summer of 2008 Parker started a newspaper for kids called *The Haller Gazette.* He is the editor-in-chief of a monthly publication that is mailed to kids in twenty-eight states.

To learn more about us, visit www.reesehaller.com and www.parkerhaller.com.

To learn more about the Statue of Responsibility, visit www.SORFoundation.org.

THE POINT OF OUR BOOK

We wrote this book so that you could know the things we do that help us be who we want to be. We want you to know that you don't have to wait to be a grown-up to be who you want to be. You can start now. You can be successful now. We think *101 Success Tips for Kids* is a good place to start.

HOW OUR BOOK IS SET UP

We divided our success tips into nine sections for easy reading. Section I, "Attitude," has twenty tips about how thinking and feelings will play an important part in your success.

Section II, "Etiquette," is about how using your manners and being polite helps others see you working at being a successful kid. You may not like it, but how people think about you when they first see you or meet you does matter. So since it matters and you know it, then do something about it. In this section we give you tips about what to do.

Section III, "Responsibility," is loaded with tips on how to be a responsible person. You will have to take responsibility for your success. No one else can do it for you. Grown-ups will help you get there, but you still have to do it.

Section IV, "Health," is the largest section, with twenty-seven tips for being a healthy kid. We think that being successful at being healthy is the most important. This was the easiest section for us to write because our family focuses on living healthy. We just wrote down the stuff we do all the time.

Section V, "Problem Solving," has tips for helping you get past the struggles that come up from time to time. Problems happen, and we help you to avoid some and find solutions to others.

Section VI, "Safety," is about having fun and being safe. We're still kids, and kids want to play and have fun. Our tips will help you do both.

Section VII, "Interaction," has tips for being around friends, family, teachers and adults you don't even know. Successful people have a group of people that they can call when they need help. As kids, we need to know how to interact with other people so we can get a group that will help us too.

Section VIII, "Language," has lots of tips about the language of success. What you say and how you say it really matters. Our dad wrote a couple of books on the importance of talk so we thought we should have a section on talking in our book too.

Section IX, "Risk," is the shortest section, with only three tips about being who you want to be now. We decided to put it at the end because it's really not all that risky being who you want to be now when you've followed all our other tips.

WHERE TO START

The most important first step is to decide to be successful. No one can tell you what being successful means for you. It can be anything. Maybe you want to become successful at making friends at school and balancing that with your schoolwork. Maybe you want to be successful at getting up in the morning using your own alarm clock. Maybe you want to be successful at multiplication or speaking up for yourself or tying your shoes. Whatever it is, we probably have a tip that will help you reach that goal.

It's time to get started. You can start reading anywhere. Just flip the book open and read the tip you land on. Some people like to pick a section and start reading at the beginning of it. Others just start with tip number one and then number two and keep going in order. You pick.

Choose a couple of tips to practice. You're probably doing some already. Share a tip with a friend or an adult. Let everyone know that being successful isn't as hard as they think.

Keep going. Soon there will be another successful kid, YOU.

SECTION I

ATTITUDE

SUCCESS TIP # 1
TAKE RESPONSIBILITY FOR YOUR ACTIONS

This is the first success tip because all the other tips won't matter if you don't take the attitude, "I am responsible for my own actions." It is time to stop blaming others for what is happening to you in your life and start looking at what you can change or do differently to have the life you want.

So be responsible for your actions. When you do something you should not have done, don't say, "He started it," or "She told me to do it." That's called "excuse making." Yeah, well, you did it too, or at least played some part in it. So no more excuses!

If you truly want to be successful, take the responsibility for reaching that goal or overcoming that problem.

SUCCESS TIP # 2
SET GOALS

What do you want to be successful at? In order to know if you are heading in the direction you want, it helps to set a goal. The goal gives you a direction and helps you stay focused. If you are going to take a vacation, you first pick where you want to go. Then you can think about how to get there, like driving or flying, and what you need to take with you, like clothes, or a swimsuit, or your passport. The goal is the target to aim at. Once you know the spot to aim for, you can line up the shot.

Imagine trying to play soccer but not knowing which goal is the one your team is defending and which one is where your team can score. The game would be in chaos, with players from both teams running in every direction. But once the goal is clear, your team can create a plan on how to pass the ball up the field and take a shot on goal.

You can set goals for the day, for the week, for the school year, for the summer. You can choose to set a goal for a weekend or for the next five years.

Successful kids set goals all the time.

SUCCESS TIP # 3
LEARN FROM YOUR MISTAKES

Everybody makes mistakes. Our dad says that making a mistake is what you do along the way to learning how to get it right. It's okay to make a mistake because it is a clue to how to act or think differently next time.

Have you ever put a puzzle together and put every piece exactly in the correct spot the first time? Probably not. You probably tried several pieces and even rotated the pieces around to get them to fit. The piece that didn't fit gave you an idea, a clue, of what piece might fit better next time.

Look at your mistakes. Don't ignore them. Talk about them, use them, learn from them.

SUCCESS TIP # 4
USE WHAT YOU DON'T WANT TO FIND WHAT YOU DO WANT

"Don't" is negative and keeps us looking away from our goal. Inside every "don't" is a "do." Flip the "don't" over and focus on the "do" side of life. "I don't want to go to bed" can be flipped around to be "I want to stay up a little bit later." "I don't want to have so much homework" can be changed into "I want to get my work done at school."

Let's say that you don't like being tickled and your dad tickles you all the time (like our dad does). If you say, "I don't want to be tickled all the time," that is not being very clear as to how you do want to be touched or when you would like to play a tickle game.

Say what you want and use your "don't wants" to discover what that is. One way our mom helps us do this is by writing down ten things we don't want on one side of a piece of paper. She then takes one at a time and talks to us about what we do want that is the opposite of the "don't." Mom writes down what we do want on the other half of the paper, going down the list one at a time. Later she cuts the paper in half and throws away the "don't want" side. Now we have a list of what we want, and then we work on ways to get those.

SUCCESS TIP # 5
MAKE A "BE" CHOICE

This is our dad's favorite saying. Every time we go out to eat he asks each of us how we are going to choose to "be" while in the restaurant. "Are you going to choose to be patient and wait for your order?" "Are you going to choose to be polite and say please and thank you to those serving us?" "Are you going to be interactive and carry on conversations with those at the table?" How you choose to be will affect the experience you're having.

So here are some questions for you to ask yourself:

How am I going to choose to be at school today? Angry, excited, bored?
How do I choose to be now that we lost the soccer match?
How do I choose to be when my little sister is crying in the car?
How do I choose to be when my best friend says, "I don't want to play with you"?
How am I am going to choose to be at gymnastic practice today?
How am I going to choose to be at my dad's house this weekend?

Make a choice and BE it!

SUCCESS TIP # 6
BE WHO YOU WANT TO BE NOW

You can do whatever you want NOW! You don't have to wait to be a grown-up. You have a contribution to make to the world right now. If you want to be a teacher, start now by helping a friend with their math or spelling. If you want to be an artist, take painting/drawing classes or clay classes if you prefer to sculpt. If you like to ride your bike, join a biking group in your state and take trips with them. If you like to sing, join the church choir. If you like to act, try out for a school play or get involved with the local acting club. If you like animals and want to be a veterinarian, volunteer at the local zoo or animal shelter or dog kennel.

It doesn't matter what you like to do. The point is to get started doing it now. Ask a parent or teacher to help you get started. Show them that you have an interest and they will help you take the next step.

If you work to be who you want to be now, adults will help you along the way. Trust in the adults around you. Start being who you want to be and the helpers will come.

SUCCESS TIP # 7
ACCEPT THE DIFFERENCES OF OTHERS

Like a snowflake, no two people are the same. People are different. We come in different sizes, shapes, colors, interests, abilities. So what if someone has braces or wears glasses? So what if someone is tall and skinny or short and fat? So what if someone likes to read a lot and play a musical instrument? So what if someone talks with an accent or wears a special wrap on their head? So what if someone believes there is no God or believes in many gods? So what?

You are not like anyone else. You are like you. You be you and let others be who they want to be. Accept the fact that you are different from them and they are different from you.

SUCCESS TIP # 8
SING

Have you ever listened to a cat purr while being stroked softly? They are singing for joy. All the animals of the world seem to have their own way to share joy. Birds sing in tweets, whales sing in a high-pitched whine, bees sing with a buzz of their wings, crickets sing with the strokes of their legs, frogs sing through croaks in their throats, even wolves sing with their howls in the night.

Singing is one of our mom's favorite things to do. She sings in her classroom with the kindergarten kids. She sings while driving in the car. She even sings while cleaning the house. Singing is her way off letting out joy.

Find your way to sing. When you're feeling happiness, let it out. Sing!

SUCCESS TIP # 9
PEOPLE ARE MORE IMPORTANT THAN RULES

Too many people are caught up in rules and regulations. They place more importance on following the guidelines written in a book than on considering what is best for the person. They forget about feelings and the needs of an individual. They ignore the important connection to people.

When we had a new wood floor put in our kitchen and dining room, Mom said that we could no longer wear shoes in the house. But after about a week we noticed that the floor was slippery and some people were slipping and falling. We sat down as a family to see what we could do about the problem and how we could keep people safe. We decided to change the rule and get shoes that people could wear in the house.

Later that day we all went shopping for a variety of shoes and house slippers that had grip soles. We bought ten different sizes of house shoes so we had enough for anybody who came to our house.

Sometimes rules need to be closely observed to see if they are what is best for the people using them. Some rules need to be changed or even no longer used because they are not what is best for the people involved.

SUCCESS TIP # 10
THE COMPUTER IS A TOOL

Too many people use the computer for playing games only. The computer is first a tool. It is a tool to help us search for information on the Internet, a tool to help us write, a tool to help us create graphic art or pictures or movies.

There is nothing wrong with using the computer as a toy and playing computer games and having fun with it. As kids we have grown up with computers and we need to remember that they can help us be successful, especially when we use them for more than just play.

SUCCESS TIP # 11
DREAM BIG DREAMS

Close your eyes for a minute and think about what life would be like if you could be whoever you wanted to be, have whatever you wanted to have, go wherever you wanted to go. Use your imagination and let your thoughts go wild. It is in your huge imagination where you find more.

At the age of sixteen, Jesse Reno dreamt about hundreds of people being lifted into the air and placed on the floor above. In his imagination he created a moving walkway that could carry people from one level to the next. Guess what Jesse invented. His invention first started out as an amusement park ride for Coney Island. It later became the escalator.

It takes no more energy or effort to imagine, to dream, to think bigger. You never know where your thoughts will take you.

SUCCESS TIP # 12
STAY FOCUSED

We had a problem with our DVD player while watching a movie. Halfway through the movie the picture got dark and fuzzy. It was hard to make out all the details and really enjoy the movie.

That is the same with setting goals. If you don't stay focused on what you want and how you plan to get it, the process of getting what you want becomes no fun. When you set a goal, get clear about what you want and stick to it. One way to do that is to cut pictures of what you want out of a magazine and glue them to a board. Our dad calls it a vision board. Then we look at the board every day and think about what we are working on getting.

Don't get sidetracked by people telling you, "You're too young," "You're just a kid," "You can have those things when you're older."

Successful people don't let other people tell them that they can't. They figure out a way no matter what other people say.

Go for it. Accomplish your dreams.

SUCCESS TIP # 13
BE OPEN TO NEW IDEAS

Some people are afraid of change. They don't want to do it differently. They want it to stay the way it has always been. Their fear keeps them from changing.

If you want to grow and reach your goals, you have to stretch yourself and do the things you haven't done before. Be open to new ideas and accept change as a way to grow.

Look at new ideas as part of your growing.

SUCCESS TIP # 14
NEVER PASS UP AN OPPORTUNITY

This is one of the tips that came from Uncle Lou. He says, "Never pass up an opportunity to go to the bathroom." It's a good idea to go to the bathroom whenever you have the opportunity to go, even if you think you don't have to go. That way you won't get caught having to "go" when there is no bathroom around.

But as a success tip, there is another meaning. Successful people take every opportunity to do what they are good at doing. They never pass up an opportunity to work on their goal or idea. They like talking about their goal, hanging around with people who have the same ideas as they do, and teaching other people how to reach similar goals.

When you take every opportunity possible to do what you love, others will see your excitement and want to be a part of it too. Never pass up an opportunity to show someone what you like to do, what you're really good at, or what your goals are.

The only time to pass up an opportunity is when someone is too negative or not very supportive. Then pass them by and just show someone else.

SUCCESS TIP # 15
SAVOR THE FLAVOR

Parker came up with the title of this tip because he likes this one a lot. This tip is not just about food, although it's a good tip when eating too. Slow down and enjoy what you are eating. Also slow down and enjoy the steps you're taking to reach your goal.

Savor the flavor is just a fun way to say enjoy the moment. Instead of thinking about what you have to do next, enjoy what is happening while it's happening.

When we were writing this book, we would take one success tip and brainstorm all kinds of silly things to say about it. We would tell jokes about it. Our dad would tell a story about when he was a boy that had something to do with the tip. Our grandpa would read us a cartoon or two that seemed to be about that tip. Our mom would tell us something funny that happened at kindergarten that was about that tip.

We savored the flavor with each success tip. Find a way to do the same with your success.

SUCCESS TIP # 16
TRUST YOUR GUT

Reese's first book, *Fred the Mouse™: The Adventures Begin*, is all about how a little mouse learns to listen carefully to his intuition. The mouse, Fred, takes time to listen, look and smell before running off into the field. He trusts himself and what he feels is the right thing to do.

We have to learn to do the same thing, to stop and check our feelings. We know what's the right thing to do, and our feelings will let us know if we are doing it or not. At our house we say, "Check it out inside." You might have heard people say, "Give it the tummy test," "Trust your gut," "Listen to your inner self."

It doesn't matter what you call it. It matters that you take the time to become aware of how you are feeling. When something doesn't feel right, then it is probably not the right thing to do.

SUCCESS TIP # 17
PLAY TO PLAY... NOT TO WIN

When we play games at our house, we play to enjoy the game and be with everyone else. If we happen to win, then that is an added plus. Our mom does this really well. She loses almost every game that we play. She smiles and laughs and enjoys the game and being a part of what is happening. She doesn't even seem to mind that she loses. She will even play again right away.

Have fun with what you choose to do, enjoy those around you, and play just to play the game.

SUCCESS TIP # 18
BE HAPPY

This tip sounds like an easy one. Be happy. It is easy to say. Our mom even sings a catchy song about being happy. Happiness is a feeling. Happiness is a choice. You can choose to be happy whenever you want. It is important to remember that your happiness is under your control.

Some people believe that things can "make" them happy. So they are always trying to get just the right thing. If they do, they are happy for a little while and then they need to get something else. When happiness is attached to a thing, you don't have as much control of it.

You can choose to be happy about things, like trading cards or a new toy. You can also choose to be happy about the things you already have. Or you can choose to just be happy. It doesn't matter as long as you keep your happiness your choice.

SUCCESS TIP # 19
GIVE

Reese wrote about giving in *Fred the Mouse™ Book Four: Giving and Receiving.* Giving and receiving are the same thing. Giving to someone is really a gift for both of you. The other person receives your gift and you receive a good feeling inside from giving. It feels good to give and to receive.

When you give, give to others because you want to, not because you will get something back. You do get the good feeling of knowing that you helped someone else, but do not expect something in return.

In our family we give all the time. We have a charity jar that we put money in and then pick a place to give it to when the jar is full. We both get money from the books we write and we give a portion of it to charity every month.

We even set up treasure hunts for each other with hints that send us on a chase all over the house, and the last clue is where we have hidden a gift for each other. It wasn't a holiday or a birthday. It was a "just because" day, and we felt good about sharing and giving. We all had fun too!

SUCCESS TIP # 20
BE THANKFUL

Be thankful for what you already have.

We said earlier that things cannot make you happy. Instead of being happy for things, be thankful for things. Every night when our mom finishes reading to us we each share one thing we are thankful for that happened during the day. Sometimes it is something little, like seeing a bright yellow finch on our bird feeder or a chance to take a bike ride on the rail trail or the lunch at school was tasty.

Take a moment right now to think about what you have. Pick one or two of them and let yourself be thankful and glad you have them. When you are thankful for the things you have, toys, family, a home, your health, then good things are returned to you. More good things come to you when you're thankful.

Be thankful not to get more but to just be thankful. How to get more is a different success tip.

SECTION II

ETIQUETTE

SUCCESS TIP # 21
SAY "PLEASE" and "THANK YOU"

Manners, manners, manners. Mom says, "Manners matter." We think saying it like that is a tongue twister. Lots of things seem to matter. It matters what you wear. It matters what you look like. It matters what you sound like. It matters when you use your manners.

Some people say that the word "please" is a magic word. Say "please" and you can have what you want. Many kids use it like "Open Sesame" or "Abracadabra," expecting to get what they want right away.

Saying "please" shows good manners, and people are more likely to help you when you use it. But the truth about the so-called magic word is that there is no guarantee that you will get what you want when you use it. It only increases your chances.

How you say "please" is an important part of this success tip. Practice saying "please" back and forth with your brother or sister or friend. Say "please" in a bossy way, a whiny way, a sarcastic way. Then try a sincere "please." Which way sounds the best? When you hear it the sincere way, don't you want to help the person who said it?

Saying, "Thank you," honors the person who just helped you. It lets them know that they are appreciated. Doesn't it feel good when someone looks into your eyes and says, "Thank you"? People remember that feeling, and you will increase the odds of them helping you in the future.

The next time you want something, remember to say, "Please," and when you get what you want say, "Thank you."

SUCCESS TIP # 22
USE YOUR NAPKIN

Napkins are wonderful things. They can clean up a mess with just a wipe and a swipe. Your sleeves on your shirt are wonderful things. They can clean up a mess with just a wipe and a swipe too.

The difference is, with one you look like you are ready to handle being a successful kid, and with the other you just have more laundry to do.

SUCCESS TIP # 23
CHEW WITH YOUR MOUTH CLOSED

Ugh! Have you ever seen someone chewing with their mouth open? It's disgusting. It is lazy eating. Manners matter! Chewing with your mouth closed is not hard to do, it just takes remembering to do it. To help us remember, Mom wrote, "I chew with my mouth closed" on a little 3x5 card and placed it standing up in front of us at the table. From time to time during the meal she would gently tap the card as a reminder instead of interrupting by saying, "Parker (or Reese), please chew with your mouth closed."

Sometimes we practice eating out at fancy restaurants. We pretend we are in Paris, France, having a meal at a five-star restaurant. We act like we're ordering in French. We use a different fork for each part of the meal. And, of course, we chew with our mouths closed.

We also like to have special days at our house where we don't eat with our mouths closed. We call them "Pirate Days" or "No manners meals." It's fun to eat like a slob sometimes.

SUCCESS TIP # 24
TIE YOUR SHOES

Either tie your shoes or wear shoes that don't need to be tied, like sandals, slip-ons or ones with Velcro straps. When you wear shoes that are supposed to be tied and you don't tie them, it looks sloppy. It sends a message to others that you are the type of person who doesn't pay attention to details. It looks like you don't care. Successful people care about the messages they send with how they dress, all the way down to their shoes.

SUCCESS TIP # 25
PULL YOUR PANTS UP

Other people do not want to see your underpants. It does NOT matter how cool you or your friends think it is. Wearing your pants around your knees is gross. Schools should not have to have a rule about how to wear your pants, but they do because kids are not thinking about success, they're thinking about being "cool."

Most people don't find showing off your underwear attractive. In fact, they find it immature and repulsive. If you really want to impress someone and make an impression that helps you, then pull up your pants and go to success tip # 26.

SUCCESS TIP # 26
TUCK IN YOUR SHIRT

Professional sports teams like the NFL and NBA have rules for the players to tuck in their jerseys when they are playing. Why is that? It's because the NFL and NBA want things to look good to the people watching. They know that even while playing football or basketball, tucking in your shirt matters. It makes the game look better. It matters for those who are watching.

Do you get the idea yet? How you look to others matters. We all wish that it didn't, but it does. So if you know that it matters, do something about it. Pull up your pants and tuck in your shirt.

SUCCESS TIP # 27
CHANGE YOUR UNDERWEAR DAILY

It's gross to wear the same pair of underwear over and over again. And turning them inside out to wear again doesn't count either.

Okay, so you probably don't do that, but are you aware of the message you're sending by the clothes you put on every day? Successful people dress for success. There is the right outfit for everything. There is a time to wear shorts and sandals. There is a time to wear dress clothes and nice shoes. There is a time to wear a swimsuit and a time to wear a winter coat.

Think about the task you are going to do that day or the weather outside as you choose your clothes. Think about the message you want to send with the clothes you're choosing to wear that day.

People are watching what you wear, and your level of success can depend on wearing the right clothes at the right time. Changing your underwear is only the beginning.

SUCCESS TIP # 28
PICK YOUR NOSE . . . IN PRIVATE

Boogers are a collection of tiny dust particles that stick to the moisture in your nose. Sometimes you might have to get the boogers out so you can breathe better. Picking is a common form of booger extraction. Picking your nose in public is a habit of many kids.

Bad habit alert! Picking your nose when others can see you doing it is a bad habit. Seeing someone else pick their nose is just plain gross. Pick in private.

If you absolutely have to clear the boogers out of your nose in public, at least use a tissue. Blow out what you can and get the rest later when you're alone, please.

SECTION III

RESPONSIBILITY

SUCCESS TIP # 29
FOLLOW DIRECTIONS

Our dad says, "The directions are one person's way of how to do something, and they're usually the easiest." He tells us from time to time that we don't have to follow the directions. We used to try to put new Lego structures together without looking at the directions, and it never looked like the picture on the cover. We've decided that when we don't follow the directions we get lost, miss a step, get confused, put it together wrong and don't understand how to fix it. We end up needing to look back at the directions. Sometimes you can find your way, put a Lego set together, or figure out the answer to a problem without using the directions. Most of the time, following the directions is a good place to start.

SUCCESS TIP # 30
USE YOUR EYES

Before giving up and saying, "I can't," use your eyes. If you can't tie your shoes, watch some of the kids that can. If you can't figure out a math problem, watch someone else do it a couple of times first. If you're struggling with learning a new trick on your skateboard, watch closely as someone else does it several times. Whatever it is that you can't do, someone, somewhere, can. Find that person and watch them for a while. Success leaves clues for you to see.

SUCCESS TIP # 31
SPEND MONEY WISELY

Our Uncle Marty is a wise money spender. Uncle Marty and Aunt Jen have a big house with lots of bedrooms and bathrooms, a garage that holds four cars and a boat, a big pool, and the largest TV we have ever seen. Uncle Marty buys lots of things, but he says, "No," to buying lots of things too. Once he told Reese that money is a tool that can help you get what you want. But if you use this tool incorrectly, it can trap you and keep you from enjoying life. Uncle Marty says the key is to make sure you have the money before you decide to buy something.

We love Legos. We love to build new Lego sets and create our own Lego structures out of all the sets we have. We also love to buy Lego sets. We search through Lego magazines and online to find the sets we want for the amount of money we have. Sometimes we find a bigger, more exciting, and more expensive set. But we always make sure we shop with the money we have, not with the money we wish we had.

When we want a bigger, better, more expensive set, we save the item number and use success tip # 32.

SUCCESS TIP # 32
SAVE MONEY WISELY

Our Uncle Marty is a wise money saver. What we just said in success tip # 31 is that you have to make sure you have the money before you decide to buy something. Well, sometimes we know what we want and we don't have enough money, so we have to save it up until we do.

At the beginning of each month we both get an allowance. As soon as we get the money we put 10 percent in a savings account, 10 percent in our family charity jar, 20 percent in an investment account, and the rest, 60 percent, we spend however we want.

Uncle Marty seems to approve. So we figure we must be on the right track.

SUCCESS TIP # 33
HUG YOUR MOTHER

This success tip is about expressing love to the people around you. Our mom sings a song that says that you should get four hugs a day. That's the minimum.

Maybe you don't feel like hugging someone. That's okay. There are lots of ways to let others know that you care about them. Our big cousin Luke gives us a high five or touches knuckles together with us. Dad gives us a unique nickname that he says at special times of the day. Our Aunt Jen says, "I love you," a lot. Our Grandma Jo kisses our eyelids. That's a little weird, but we know what it means. Uncle Marty is always checking to make sure we have enough to eat or are comfortable. Bondy spends time with us every day, reading the comics to us, eating donuts together, or teaching us about flowers. Mom likes hugs. We make sure she gets at least four hugs a day.

How do the people in your life say, "I love you," or "I care about you"? Everyone has their own special way. What is your special way of expressing love? Start today. Hug your mother.

SUCCESS TIP # 34
PUT YOUR DIRTY CLOTHES IN THE LAUNDRY BASKET

Some of us at our house have trouble remembering to put our dirty clothes in the laundry basket. We're not going to name names, but we know who we're talking about. It is a simple task and it doesn't take much effort.

Did you know that your brain can think more clearly when your environment is clean and safe? Putting your clothes in the laundry basket is one way to keep your personal space more clean and safe. Our dad says it's a sign of being more responsible. When people are responsible with their personal space, they tend to be successful at being responsible with other things too.

At our house we're all helping each other get better at keeping a clean, safe and clutter-free environment.

SUCCESS TIP # 35
TURN OFF THE LIGHTS

Stop lighting the room for nobody. Save the energy by turning off the lights when you leave the room. When you save the energy, you're saving the planet. Every little bit counts.

Flick the switch!

SUCCESS TIP # 36
CLOSE THE REFRIGERATOR DOOR

Think about what you want to get out of the refrigerator before you open it. If you're not sure what you want, take a quick peak. It's not that hard to close the refrigerator door. It helps keep the food from getting moldy and saves energy. Remember, saving a little now adds up later.

The future of our planet is in our hands now. We can make a difference today. Do what you can, where you can, whenever you can. Close the refrigerator door.

SUCCESS TIP # 37
JUMP ON YOUR OWN BED

Our mom and dad tell us all the time, "Jump on your own bed." For some reason it's much more fun to jump on their bed. Their bed is bigger, you can bounce higher on it, and they have lots of pillows too. The problem is we usually create a big mess. The blankets and sheet come untucked, the pillows lose stuffing, and the bed starts to creak. Jumping on their bed is fun.

Are you wondering why this is a success tip?

Well, here's the answer. You get to have fun and make a mess, but make the mess with your own stuff. Make a mess of your own bed, your own toys, your own bike, your own grades. When you start to mess up other people's stuff, they get mad and don't like you being around them.

SUCCESS TIP # 38
FEED THE CAT
(or dog, hamster, bird, fish)

Simply put, take care of the animals around you. People, animals, and plants are the living part of our world. Let's be responsible enough to take care of all of them. If you can't be responsible enough to feed your cat or hamster or bird, then maybe you're not ready to do what it takes to be a successful kid. Maybe you're not ready to be responsible for your choices, your behavior, and your future.

Get ready by taking care of the animals you love. You'll get better at taking care of your pets and then yourself and other people.

Remember, we're just kids and all have to start somewhere. We think you learn more responsibility when you have a pet and take care of it.

SUCCESS TIP # 39
USE YOUR OWN ALARM CLOCK

Take charge of when you get up in the morning. You know when you need to get up to get ready for school or ready for swim practice or volleyball practice. It's not your mom's job to get you up. It is your mom's job to help you buy an alarm clock and teach you how to use it.

We have both been using our alarm clocks and getting up by ourselves since the first grade. So we know you can do it too.

SECTION IV
HEALTH

SUCCESS TIP # 40
SWING

We love to swing. It is a way to relax and let your mind go calm. Some people call relaxing the mind "meditation." It doesn't matter what you call it as long as you do it. Sometimes we relax our minds on the swing and sometimes we relax our minds in the hot tub. It doesn't matter where you choose to relax your mind as long as you pick a place where you can actually do it.

Relaxing your mind is important for kids because it helps to clear your mind of junk and clutter. When you relax your mind it's easier to think of new ideas or things to do. We get great writing ideas when we are calm and quiet.

Parker came up with the idea of a newspaper for kids to keep kids reading in the summer while sitting in the hot tub. We now have a newspaper called *The Haller Gazette* that is mailed to kids in twenty-eight states. If you want to receive your free copy of *The Haller Gazette*, e-mail your name and postal address to parker@thomashaller.com.

SUCCESS TIP # 41
READ

Reading is one of our favorite things to do. We take books with us wherever we go. It's fun to read and think about being in a different, imaginary world. We each read about a book a week. You read the way that fits you best.

The key is to read what you know you like, not what other people think you should like. Ask a librarian to help you pick out a few books on topics you're interested in most. If you're not sure what you like, start anywhere. Read magazines, comics, short stories, history, science, science fiction, or self-help books like this one. Read for pleasure and enjoyment or read for knowledge.

Read.

SUCCESS TIP # 42
WRITE

Benjamin Franklin once said, "Do things worth writing, write things worth reading." Writing is a good way to capture your ideas and share your thoughts with others. It's a way to remember the day that has just passed or a trip you just took. It's a way to express yourself and let the world know what you think is important. It's a way to give people important information.

You can write to yourself in a private journal. You can write on the back of a photo to remember the event. You can write a letter to your grandma. You can write an instant message to a friend on your computer. You can write a message to your best friend on your cell phone.

You can write one sentence that describes your summer vacation. You can write a short story for a writing contest. You can write a research paper about plants or butterflies. You can write a book about a mouse that lives in your barn. You can write a book about a pig that goes to space. You can write about whatever you want.

SUCCESS TIP # 43
PLAY

Play is important and it is also a way to learn. We can learn new things by trying them out in play. Play is a way to act out some of the things we might want to do later as an adult. Play exercises your body too. Sometimes it is fun to play in the sand or swing or build with blocks. Other times it is fun to play like you're a firefighter or a schoolteacher or a doctor. Play like you're a police officer or business owner or professional basketball player. Play like you're a chef in a fancy restaurant or a painter or a farmer. It doesn't matter as long as you're having fun.

Adults should play too. They should play and act like kids. Not all the time but enough so that they're not working so much.

Keep life fun. Play!

SUCCESS TIP # 44
TAKE YOUR MEDICINE

Kids don't like to take medicine, but to stay healthy you have to take it sometimes. Most people, kids and adults, don't like taking medicine. But being sick is even worse. Medicine is used to help you. If you don't take it, it can't help. So take it even if it is gross.

Parker has lots of allergies and has to take two different medicines twice a day. Neither of us likes to take medicine, but we take it so we can stay healthy and do more of the things we like to do.

SUCCESS TIP # 45
COUGH IN YOUR SLEEVE

Parker's preschool teacher, Beth, taught him this important health tip. A few years later we were at the family doctor getting our vaccinations for school when we saw a big poster on the wall in the waiting room. It gave all the reasons why people should stop coughing in their hands and start coughing in their sleeves.

When you cough in your hands, you pass on the germs from your hands to the things you touch. When you cough in your sleeve, you won't pass on as many germs to other people. The germs get caught on your sleeve and they have nowhere to go.

Those Montessori schoolteachers sure do know a lot.

SUCCESS TIP # 46
RECYCLE

When you recycle, you save the planet. Just because you're a kid doesn't mean that you can't do your part in saving the environment. You're part of this world now. So act now to keep it clean. It's not that hard to do. It's as easy as one - two - three.

One: Create a space for a recycling bin or container.

Two: Create a time each day when the family puts something in the bin. At our house the recycle bin time is when we're cleaning the dishes after supper. We're already working together to keep our kitchen environment clean and we can keep the world clean this way too.

Three: Make a commitment to do it and follow through.

SUCCESS TIP # 47
CLEAN YOUR ROOM

The success tip we wrote before this one is about keeping the environment clean by recycling, and this tip is similar. It's about keeping your personal environment clean. We're talking about your bedroom.

Keeping your room clean helps you in lots of ways. An environment that is not full of clutter helps your mind to not be filled with clutter too. You can be more relaxed and imagine things better in a place that is safe and comfortable.

Another way that a clean room can help you is if you have allergies or get sick easily. Microscopic bugs like dust mites and bedbugs love clutter. The more clutter there is the more they can grow. The more tiny bugs there are in your room the more your body has to work to keep you healthy. This takes time and energy away from the important kid tasks of being creative and using your imagination.

Nobody likes to clean their room, but they always feel better when it's done.

SUCCESS TIP # 48
BRUSH YOUR TEETH IN THE MORNING

Did you know that at night ten billion bacteria climb into your mouth and begin to eat away at your teeth? If you leave them, they continue to dig at your teeth. Then when you eat breakfast, you push that bacteria further into the holes they have been creating.

Get that yuck off your teeth and out of your mouth right away when you wake up in the morning.

Most people usually go to the bathroom to use the toilet right away in the morning. While you're in there, you might as well brush your teeth too.

SUCCESS TIP # 49
ONLY BRUSH THE TEETH YOU WANT TO KEEP

We learned this one from Uncle Lou. One night while Uncle Lou and Uncle Barb (Yes, for some reason we call his wife Uncle Barb - don't asks us why, it was something from when we were little.) Anyway . . . they were visiting our house and we were complaining about getting ready for bed and having to brush our teeth. Uncle Lou quickly commented, "Hey, only brush the teeth you want to keep."

It took us a minute to think about what he was saying. Was Uncle Lou giving us permission to not brush our teeth? At first we thought, "Wow, we don't have to brush our teeth anymore!" As we were walking up the stairs to go to bed, we both looked at each other and almost at the same time said, "Hey, I want to keep all my teeth."

We laughed at each other and headed straight to the bathroom. Yes, we both decided to keep the teeth we already have. We think you should too.

SUCCESS TIP # 50
WASH YOUR HANDS

Millions of germs are passed from your hands to the things you touch and from the things you touch to your hands. Once the germs are on your hands, you touch your face, eyes and mouth. The germs enter your body and BAM you're sick.

Our mom has a big container of hand cleaner in her kindergarten classroom. She has the kinderkids wash their hands several times a day. She also has a special traveling hand washer for us in her car. She makes sure her hands are clean before coming home. You never know what her hands have touched. Boy, we're glad she washes her hands a lot.

SUCCESS TIP # 51
TAKE A SHOWER OR A BATH

You may not be able to see the dirt on your body, but it's there. You may not be able to smell yourself, but other people can. You may not care how you look or smell, but it matters to the people around you, especially if you're in the sixth grade or higher.

It's fun to play and get dirty. As kids, we're going to get dirty. That's okay. In the spring, when our horse's riding arena turns to mud, we love to run through it barefoot. Sometimes we fall and end up covered in mud. It's fun getting dirty.

You probably have something fun that you like to do where you end up dirty too. Just remember that whether you get dirty a little bit or a lot (like we do in the riding arena), being a successful kid means that you take care of your body by keeping it clean.

SUCCESS TIP # 52
GET YOUR HOMEWORK DONE

What are you waiting for? If you know you have schoolwork to complete at home, why wait until the last minute to get it done? When you wait until later, your brain holds onto knowing it has something more to do. This can become stressful for your body. You also run the risk of running out of time and having to rush through your work.

Change how you think about homework. If you continue to think of it as terrible and awful, then that is how it will always be for you. Instead, start thinking of homework as practice time. It is the time you set aside to practice the things that will help you continue to be successful as you grow. You practice soccer so you can get better at it and have more fun during the game. You practice gymnastics or swimming or basketball the same way, right? Think of your schoolwork the same way. It's practice that helps make life easier and more fun later.

You have a time to practice soccer or basketball. You have a time to eat. You have a time to go to bed. Do the same with your homework. Pick a time every day to do your homework. We like to have something to eat right after school and relax for about a half hour, and then get started on schoolwork. We call the time of day where we do our school work "grow the brain time," because that is exactly what we are doing, growing our brains.

SUCCESS TIP # 53
DO THE MATH

Math is everywhere. It's in everything. Cell phones, computers, video games, movies, basketball, baseball, soccer, gymnastics, bicycles, skateboards are all influenced by math. You name it and math probably has something to do with it. Math is a part of science. It's a part of history. It's a part of art, and it's a part of nature. The more you understand math, the more you will understand the world. The more comfortable you are with using math, the more comfortable you will be when using the things that help you be successful.

The only way to get comfortable with math is to practice it, learn it, and use it.

SUCCESS TIP # 54
GO TO SCHOOL

The more education you have, the more successful you can become. School is where we learn more about the world and how it works. Even teachers continue to go to school and learn more about being a better teacher.

Successful people are always looking for new things to learn and news ways to learn. Going to school never really ends. It just takes different forms as you get older. Uncle Marty is a doctor and he goes to conferences to learn new techniques. Uncle Lou is a professor at a university and he says that he attends seminars and workshops to learn more. Our dad goes to three or four conferences every year to learn new ideas about writing and selling books. Bondy is retired and takes classes at the community college just for fun. Mom takes classes every summer when she is not teaching kindergarten.

Learning takes many forms. For kids it takes the form of school. Keep growing, keep learning and keep going to school.

SUCCESS TIP # 55
TURN OFF THE TV

TV is junk food for your mind. It's like potato chips or french fries or soda pop. It has very little in it to help you grow. There are educational programs on TV but most kids don't watch those on a regular basis.

Watching too much TV is not good for you. Just like eating junk food all the time is not good for you. You can have some junk food from time to time and you can have some TV from time to time.

Keep your TV watching to just a little bit.

SUCCESS TIP # 56
GET UP BEFORE 10 A.M.

No need to waste the day. Get up and get going. Some of the most peaceful times in the day are early in the morning. Reese wrote his *Fred the Mouse*™ book series in the morning, getting up at about six o'clock, when the house was quiet and calm. Parker loves to get up early and read while snuggling under a big blanket.

There is something we like about the morning. Perhaps when you experience the quietness of the morning, you will like it too.

SUCCESS TIP # 57
GO TO BED EARLY

Benjamin Franklin should probably get credit for this success tip. He said, "Early to bed, early to rise, makes a man healthy, wealthy, and wise." We figured if Benjamin Franklin did it, then we would do it too.

Guess what, it works! We feel so much better when we get enough rest, which is about nine to ten hours a night. Going to bed early helps us get the rest we need, and it will help you too.

SUCCESS TIP # 58
EXERCISE

More and more kids are having health problems because of being overweight and out of shape. Kids are eating too much junk food and fast food and sitting around playing video games and watching TV.

Our bodies are made to move. Find something that you like to do that requires you to move: skateboarding, biking, any sport, even walking. Keep your body healthy with some kind of exercise.

SUCCESS TIP # 59
DRINK WATER

Our bodies are mostly made of water, and what they need put into them is fresh, clean water. It keeps your body hydrated and running. Soda pop is the triple whammy of junk for your body: caffeine, sugar, and carbonation. If you drink a diet pop, you end up putting a bunch of other chemicals in your body that are no better than sugar. Sports drinks are tasty and better for you than pop and "energy" drinks, but water is still the best.

Treat soda pop and any kind of sugar drink exactly like junk food, because that is what it is, junk for your body. Have some soda pop and keep it limited. No need for the super-big-size drink. You don't sit down to eat a super-big-size bag of potato chips all at once.

Soda pop is no different. Have some junk, but not a lot.

Keep it simple, drink water.

SUCCESS TIP # 60
STAY AWAY FROM CAFFEINE

Kids like to drink energy drinks loaded with caffeine. You can even buy little tiny cans of liquid caffeine to add to any drink you want. This is craziness. Caffeine is bad for your body. It's a drug that affects your body on the inside.

Stay clean, stay pure, stay away from caffeine.

SUCCESS TIP # 61
EAT THE RAINBOW

Eat the rainbow!! "How can I do that?" you ask. It's easy. Foods come in all different colors: red, orange, yellow, green, blue and purple, just like the colors in the rainbow. Eat foods with a wide variety of color. Bright colorful foods are healthier for your body. Below is a list of the colorful foods we like to eat. The list is small because we don't like everything. Here are some of our favorites that we eat:

RED	ORANGE	YELLOW	GREEN	BLUE	PURPLE
Apples	Peppers	Apples	Apples	Blueberries	Grapes
Strawberries	Oranges	Bananas	Broccoli	Blueberries	Eggplant
Cherries	Melons	Peppers	Peas	Blueberries	Cabbage
Raspberries	Cauliflower		Grapes	Blueberries	
Watermelon	Carrots			Blueberries	

Can you tell our two favorite fruits to eat? Hint: one is blue and the other is in three color categories. Each member in our family has a list like this. Mom's is smaller than ours and Dad's is three times bigger.

What does your list look like?

SUCCESS TIP # 62
EAT BREAKFAST

Breakfast is the most important meal of the day. Eating breakfast gets your body's furnace going in the morning. Did you know that studies show that kids who eat a healthy breakfast remember things better and do better in school?

The key to eating breakfast is eating a healthy one. Most cereal is nothing more that puffed sugar. We love it and don't eat it as a breakfast meal. The "puffed sugar" cereals are what we put into the junk food category. We eat some but not a lot.

Eat breakfast, and make it a healthy one when you do.

SUCCESS TIP # 63
CREATE MEMORIES and KEEP THEM SPECIAL

Whenever we take a family trip, our goal is to create memories. It doesn't matter if we go on a long trip or a bike ride on the rail trail. We're out to create a memory, capture it on camera, collect a meaningful trinket when possible, talk about it in the car on the way home, write about it when we get home, and tell stories about it later.

Do things that you have never done before so that you will have great memories and wonderful stories to tell when you're done. Along the way collect stickers, rocks, stamps, coins or anything that helps keep the memory special.

SECTION V
PROBLEM SOLVING

SUCCESS TIP # 64
THERE IS MORE THAN ONE WAY TO SOLVE A PROBLEM

Our dad says, "You always have more options than you think."

It's harder to solve a problem if you're not open to listening to as many solutions as possible. You're full of ideas, and so are all the people around you. If you think your idea is the only one, then you limit your options and maybe even your success.

Stay open to new, different or even unusual solutions to the problems you face. When you do, you'll discover new ways to be successful.

SUCCESS TIP # 65
CREATE A SYSTEM

A system helps you do things in order. When you create an order to your work, you save yourself time and energy. Before getting started at doing anything, think about what would be the best order to do it in.

When we unload the dishwasher, we stop and think about who's going to work on the right side and who's on the left. Who is going to put the glasses away and who's doing the plates? It's the same with putting the dirty dishes in. It only takes a few seconds to figure it out together, and within minutes the job is done and we're off to playing and having fun.

SUCCESS TIP # 66
ASK FOR HELP

You may not get what you want unless you ask. Asking is a way to let others know that you need help or want something. We don't have a glass head. People can't see our thoughts and figure out what we want or need. Asking helps our wants to become more visible to others. There is no guarantee that you will get what you ask for, but it increases your chances.

You won't know until you ask. You won't know who will be able to help you unless you ask for help. You won't know if you can have the toy you want or the chance to stay up later or a chance to play if you don't ask.

Others won't know you need help if you don't ask. If you don't ask your teacher to explain the math problem you are struggling with, she doesn't know you need help. If you don't ask your soccer coach for a chance to play offense, he doesn't know you want to be on offense. If you don't ask the person standing on your foot to get off, they may never realize that they are standing on your foot.

Successful kids are comfortable with asking for help or for what they want.

SUCCESS TIP # 67
OFFER TO HELP

Pay attention to what's going on around you. When you see some-one struggling with something, offer to help. You never know when someone might need an extra hand. You can hold open a door, pick up a pencil that just fell on the floor, search for a missing item in their locker, or give directions on how to get to a classroom.

Helping someone else is an act that shows you care about other people.

Successful kids are comfortable with offering to help.

SUCCESS TIP # 68
THINK AHEAD

This success tip is about thinking about the results of something before it happens. Our dad calls it thinking from the end first. When you think ahead, or from the end first, you're thinking about your choices and what could happen because of the choices you make.

Have you ever said, "I didn't mean for that to happen"? Well, you probably didn't mean it, but did you think about what could happen first or did you just go racing into it? When you don't think about what could happen next, you run the risk of being out of control and causing things to happen that you really didn't want to happen.

Successful kids stop and think along the way because they know that when they think ahead they have more control over their choices.

SUCCESS TIP # 69
PREPARE THE NIGHT BEFORE

Get ready. Be prepared. If you know what is coming, then get ready for it early so you don't have to be rushed at the last minute. When you are in a hurry and rush to get ready, you are more likely to forget something or make a mistake.

Set your school clothes out before you go to bed. Pack your book bag the night before. Get your soccer bag packed with all you need for game day. Look through your homework and double check to make sure it's all there before you go to sleep.

When you're prepared the night before, your mind is free to relax and have a peaceful night's rest.

SUCCESS TIP # 70
CHECK YOURSELF

CHECK YOURSELF is printed in big letters on a board next to the door where we leave the house every morning. It is there to remind us to check one last time and make sure we have everything we need for school or practice. We've learned that our mom and dad are not going to go back and get something we left behind. We've learned this because there was a time when we didn't check ourselves and we didn't have what we needed. We've left our shoes at home and had to wear our snow boots all day in school. We've left our lunch and had to eat yucky school lunch. We've left our homework and received a grade we didn't want to get. We've left lots behind and learned that it's easier to check yourself before you leave.

Make sure you have everything you need before you leave. There is one last opportunity to check yourself. Use it.

SECTION VI
SAFETY

SUCCESS TIP # 71
BE SAFE

It's important to have fun, play and enjoy life. While you're playing, keep in mind to do it safely. You don't want to be so careful that you're not having fun, and you don't want to be so wild that you or others get hurt. Balance fun with safety.

SUCCESS TIP # 72
BUCKLE YOUR SEAT BELT

This is a no-brainer. When the car stops quickly, things inside continue to move forward. If you don't strap those things down, they could fly right through the front windshield. If that something is you, then you're the thing flying through the front windshield.

Our mom, grandma, and grandpa (Bondy) were in a serious car accident when our mom was younger. The seat belts they were wearing saved their lives. We are not going to risk our lives and you shouldn't either.

Buckle up!

SUCCESS TIP # 73
WEAR YOUR BIKE HELMET

Protect your brain. The last thing you ever want is for your brain to be damaged and not work the way it is supposed to. If your head gets hit hard enough, your brain can lose the ability to remember or talk or walk or see. Everything you know and can do could be lost with one whack to the head. Falling off your bike and hitting your head could be the whack that does it. Why risk all you have learned and become? Put on your helmet!

Forget what your friends say or tease you about. Your head is worth it. Your brain is worth it. YOU are worth it.

We always wear our helmets when riding our bikes. Please wear yours too.

SUCCESS TIP # 74
PUT ON SUNSCREEN

We hate sunscreen. We hate the slimy feeling the lotion leaves on our skin. We hate the spray sunscreen and the sticky feeling it leaves behind. We put on sunscreen for one reason and one reason only, to protect our skin.

The body needs a little bit of sun. Our dad says about ten to fifteen minutes of sun every day is all we need. Too much sun might hurt your skin, now with a sunburn and later, when you're an adult, with skin cancer.

Sometimes we have to do what we don't like and even hate in order to protect ourselves, like put on sunscreen.

SUCCESS TIP # 75
WEAR SUNGLASSES

Sunglasses are like sunscreen for the eyes. They keep your inner eye and your eyelids from getting burned by filtering out the harmful rays of the sun. Wear sunglasses even on cloudy days, because those harmful rays still go through the clouds.

SUCCESS TIP # 76
PROTECT YOUR EARS

Protect what you have now, good hearing, and save it for later. Wear earplugs when you mow the grass, go to the movie theater, or attend a music concert. Turn the volume down on your stereo, video game and television.

Protect your hearing now so you can have the hearing of a twelve-year-old when you're fifty.

SUCCESS TIP # 77
LEARN TO SWIM

Playing in the water is fun. It's a blast to splash in a pool, dive for coins, zoom down giant slides, tube at the lake, water ski, and lounge on a floaty. And it's dangerous if you don't know how to swim.

Take lessons. Get comfortable with putting your face in the water. Learn a few swimming strokes. You don't have to become Michael Phelps, but at least learn how to move through the water doing something other than the dog paddle.

SUCCESS TIP # 78
KEEP SAND BELOW THE KNEES

Do you know what can happen when you throw sand? It can hurt someone by getting in their mouth, eyes or ears. We have a big sandpile in our backyard to play in, and it's the rule to keep sand below the knees. It's easier to remember when you say it this way instead of "Don't throw sand."

We added this statement to our success tips because it's really about how your actions affect others. Throwing sand can really hurt someone else, and you have to think about that before you start throwing. Name-calling can really hurt someone, and you have to think about that before you start shouting. Hitting and kicking can really hurt someone, and you have to think about that before you start swinging. Gossip can really hurt someone, and you have to think about that before you start talking.

Successful kids think about how their choices and actions affect not just themselves, but others too.

SECTION VII
INTERACTION

SUCCESS TIP # 79
NURTURE NATURE

Take a moment to look at how you live your life and the effect it's having on the world around you. Do you live with only yourself in mind? Do you think of yourself as more important than a tiny bug or a small rodent? Do you even think about the other creatures of the world?

How would you live differently if you were kind to all animals, respected nature, and saw the life of every living thing as special?

It's time to start living in a way that nurtures nature!

SUCCESS TIP # 80
SHARE WITH OTHERS

Sharing with others is a way to give back out of what you have been given. We have lots of things that we can share, from toys or a ball to money or opinions. Most of the time it's sharing the little things, like an idea, a seat on the bus, a piece of gum, a blanket or sweatshirt, or an umbrella that seems to matter the most.

Opportunities to share happen all around us. Open your eyes and look for them. The next time you see an opportunity to share will you . . . share?

SUCCESS TIP # 81
HELP WITH THE DISHES

We could also call this success tip, "Work Together," because that's what helping with the dishes is all about. Working together is a way to get something done faster. When we work together, it spreads out the amount of work each person has to do. The dishes get washed faster, the living room gets cleaned easier, the grass gets mowed quicker, the laundry gets finished sooner, the garage gets cleaned better, and the heavy boxes get lifted easier.

Working together is also a way to come up with more ideas and solutions when you run into a problem. Success tip # 65 is "There is more than one way to solve a problem," and when you have more brains to think about one problem, you have more ideas and solutions that come out. One person's idea gives another person an idea they didn't think about at first.

When we work together as a family, we can solve problems much faster and easier. The same is true for us at school or even as a nation. When we decide to work together, many of the world's problems can be solved faster and easier. When we work as individuals or as separate countries, we can't solve as many problems.

SUCCESS TIP # 82
PARTICIPATE

Join in, get involved, be a part, volunteer, include yourself, sign up, join the team, dive in, get out there, get off your butt, give it a whirl, take it for a spin are all different was to say, "Participate."

You can't become successful sitting around doing nothing. Participate in life and get involved with other people who are doing what you like to do.

Success comes to those who get out there, volunteer when they can, dive in when needed, and participate. Success comes to those who go after what they want.

Get up. Get moving. Success is out there.

SUCCESS TIP # 83
TOUCH EACH OTHER GENTLY

There are many ways to touch someone. You can touch someone in a physical way, like hugs, handshakes, kisses, holding hands, putting your arms around someone, hitting, kicking, biting, scratching, and poking. You can also touch someone with words of encouragement, blowing someone a kiss, thumbs up, wink, smile, yelling, screaming, cussing, gossip and rumors.

You can choose to touch someone in a physical or nonphysical way. But whichever way you choose, do it with kindness. Use kind words when you talk to others. Have peaceful thoughts when you think about others. Have a gentle touch when you reach out to someone else.

Let's all get rid of hitting, kicking, biting, scratching, screaming, cussing, and gossiping.

It is time for the people of the world to touch each other gently.

SUCCESS TIP # 84
RESPECT THE PRIVACY OF OTHERS

Will you let others have the privacy they need? If someone is mad or upset, will you let them be alone until they're ready to talk about it with you? If someone is tired, will you let them rest? Will you not look at someone else's grade on their paper unless they show you? Will you not peek into someone's book bag? Will you not search through your friend's contacts list on their cell phone? Will you not read your friend's text message or e-mail? Will you stay out of other people's business?

We all need our own space. We need to be able to be alone and sit quietly. We need a place we can call ours: a bedroom, a desk to study at, a comfortable chair, a locker for our books, coat, and boots. We need to have a place to go when we're sad or angry or just want to rest. And most importantly, we need to feel like our personal life is not being picked apart by others.

Live your life the way that is best for you and let other people live life the way that is best for them.

SUCCESS TIP # 85
SPEAK CLEARLY

Our mom tells the kindergarten kids to "Speak loud and clear so all can hear."

Your words are important, and you want people to be able to hear them. When you talk softly, with your mouth pointed at the ground, you might not be heard. Tilt your head toward the person you're talking to and look directly at them. Speak as if you're sending your words right into their ears.

At our school presentations we speak in front of five hundred to six hundred kids at a time. Our dad reminds us before every presentation to talk loud and clear to the ears of the person in the back row. He calls that "projecting." We just repeat to ourselves what our mom says: "Speak loud and clear so all can hear."

SUCCESS TIP # 86
CREATE FAMILY TIME

Family is important. Create time to be together with your family as much as possible. Do something together as a family on a regular basis - sitting and watching TV doesn't count. Do something that is about interacting with each other. Play a game, tell stories, read to each other, cook together, or enjoy a family meal.

We like to sit in the hot tub as a family and talk about the day, especially during the cold Michigan winter. Each person shares something from the day that they enjoyed, found interesting, or learned. Sometimes we talk about a problem and how to solve it. We call that special family time, "Hot Tub Time."

What could you create with your family, and how will you keep it special?

SUCCESS TIP # 87
LET OTHERS SEE YOUR WORK

There are two parts to this success tip. First, let someone else check over your work before you turn it in. The person you show it to can help you correct any mistakes before you finalize your work.

Second, when you're all finished, share your work with others. Let other people see the energy and effort you put into your creation.

It's okay to be proud of what you accomplished. Put your name on it. Sign it like a famous artist or a best-selling author. It's yours. You did it. Share it with the world.

SUCCESS TIP # 88
CHOOSE YOUR FRIENDS WISELY

Our dad says, "Your attitude is similar to the attitude of the five people you hang around the most." In other words, you act a lot like your friends.

Are the people you're hanging around with really the people that fit you the best? Be honest with yourself and ask yourself some of the following questions: Do my friends treat me kindly and help me reach my dreams? Do they talk nice about me when I'm not around? Do they help me when I'm stuck or having trouble? Are they happy for me when I'm successful? Do they stick up for me when others say hurtful things about me? Are the people I hang around really the kind of people I want to be like?

Do pick the friends you want. Just remember, you'll probably end up a lot like them. So choose wisely.

SUCCESS TIP # 89
ACT YOUR AGE

Act the way you know you should act. Kids don't have to act older than they are. When you're ten, you don't have to act like you are sixteen. When you're fifteen, do what fifteen-year-olds do. When you're twelve, be twelve.

This goes the other way too. When you're ten, don't cry and pout like a three-year-old. When you're twenty, don't act like you're a teenager. When you're an adult, act like a grown-up should act.

Be who you are, and act your age at the same time.

SECTION VIII
LANGUAGE

SUCCESS TIP # 90
REMOVE "I CAN'T" LANGUAGE

Some of the biggest ways we limit ourselves is by saying, "I can't," or "I don't know how." It's important for kids to realize that they don't always have to know what to do next. Just go with the flow and act like you do. When you think that you can't do something, act like you have done it one hundred times before. If you think that you don't know how, that's okay. Act like you do and watch what happens. As you get started, the next step often appears. Sometimes a teacher or another person gives you a tip or idea along the way.

Acting as if keeps you moving toward your goal. Remember, it's okay to make a mistake, because mistakes are clues.

Feeling stuck? Act as if, make a mistake, read the clue, make a change, and *act as if* some more.

SUCCESS TIP # 91
SPEAK KINDLY OF OTHERS

Have you ever heard the phrase, "If you don't have anything nice to say, don't say anything at all"? Our mom says it a different way. "Speak kindly of others because to speak any other way about someone is hurting them."

Talking about someone when they're not present is called gossip or spreading a rumor. Spreading rumors is one of the most hurtful things you can do to someone. It is hurtful to them even when they are not around to hear it, because the rumor affects how other people think and act toward them in the future.

If a friend is spreading rumors about someone, doesn't it make you wonder what they are saying about you when you're not around? Talking about someone "behind their back" doesn't sound like a friend.

Speak kindly of others, or maybe it's best to just let people speak for themselves and about themselves.

SUCCESS TIP # 92
TELL THE TRUTH

Be honest and truthful with your words. Everyone likes it when they can trust that what you're saying is the way it really happened. Adults like it when kids speak their mind. Just remember to do it in a kind, gentle tone.

When you don't tell the truth, people don't trust you. Getting someone to trust you after you have lied to them is hard to do, and it takes a long time to get their trust back.

Start today. Tell the truth.

SUCCESS TIP # 93
SPEAK UP FOR YOURSELF

How long do you let someone stand on your toe before you say, "Ouch, you're standing on my toe"? If you don't say something, they may never know what is happening and stand there while you stay in pain. It's time to stop being a victim to what is going on around you. Say what you feel. Ask for what you need. Share your opinion. Tell others what you think. Let your wants be known.

Remember, you don't have a glass head. No one can see your thoughts, know what you're thinking, or understand what you want or don't want unless you speak up for yourself.

SUCCESS TIP # 94
LISTEN BEFORE YOU SPEAK

Your words are important, and having them heard is what so many of us kids are trying to do every day. A key to being heard is to listen. Let people finish what they're saying before you ask a question or attempt to give your answer or opinion. People will see you as someone who is interested in them and what they have to say. They will then be more likely to listen to you when you are speaking.

When you listen first, you also find out more about what the other person is ready to hear. They might not be ready to hear what you have to say, and then they won't hear it anyway. Listen before you speak and you will then know how to respond and have what you say heard more clearly.

SUCCESS TIP # 95
<u>SAY MORE THAN "I'M SORRY"</u>

The phrase, "I'm sorry," said by itself doesn't cut it. Saying "I'm sorry" is only the beginning of what you need to say when you've hurt someone. It's not the end. "I'm sorry" should always be followed by an explanation of how you will act or what you will do differently next time. How are you planning on touching the person you hit out of anger the next time you become angry? What will you say to the person you cussed at the next time you become upset at them?

When you say what you're going to do next time, you're taking responsibility for your actions and how those actions will change so that you won't cause hurt next time and won't have to say, "I'm sorry," next time either.

SUCCESS TIP # 96
<u>SAY HOW YOU FEEL</u>

We all have four basic feelings: sad, mad, glad, and scared. Feelings are neither good nor bad. They are just feelings. Your feelings are your feelings, and it is important for you to have them and express them. When you're feeling something, it's okay to tell other people. Talk to other people who will be kind with you about how you're feeling and why you might be feeling that way. Never say, "I'm fine," unless you're actually fine. When you are not fine, say what you are feeling.

How you express your feelings is as important as having the feeling in the first place. Don't just stomp off and slam doors when you're angry. Say, "I'm angry and I need some alone time right now." When you're sad, say, "I'm sad and I feel like crying on the inside." When you're scared, get close to someone safe and say, "I'm scared." When you're happy, let others see it and hear it. Say, "I feel happy on the inside."

SUCCESS TIP # 97
STOP WHINING

Grown-ups don't like to hear whining, and other kids don't like to hear it either. It's a form of complaining, and successful people don't complain. Problems are a challenge to overcome. Whining doesn't help you overcome a problem. It keeps you focused on the problem, and the more you focus on the problem the less time you have to focus on the solution.

The problem is, whining sometimes gets you what you want. Some parents just give you what you're whining about to keep you quiet. But you never learn how to get that thing by yourself. You always need someone else to do it for you.

Remember, you're in control of your success. Other people, teachers, parents, friends are there to help, not do it for you. So if you need something, use your words and ask. Learn to become a better asker and you increase your chances of getting what you want.

SUCCESS TIP # 98
PLAY WITH WORDS

Playing with words is a fun way to learn more words. We like to play word games as a family. When we're traveling in the car, we try to come up with as many words as possible for things we see. When someone sees a bird, we shout out different names for birds, like fowl, raptor, and fine-feathered friend. When we go over a bridge, we yell out all the different ways to say "top," such as peak, crown, apex, summit, and crest.

Whatever you see, there is another way to say it. A car can be changed to automobile, vehicle, or transportation. A tree can be a plant, foliage, or underbrush.

Our dad likes to play the homograph game. This is where one word has two different meanings. For example, the word "fall" can refer to the time of year, autumn, or it can mean to tip over. When he is talking, he twists the meaning around and keeps us guessing. Most of the time it's fun, and sometimes he can get annoying.

SECTION IX
RISKS

SUCCESS TIP # 99
EXPLORE

Get out there in the world and go to new places and try new things. As kids, we need lots of experiences being in the world. It's how we figure out what we're good at and what fits us best.

Finding new things to do and new places to do them is fun, exciting, and a bit risky. Take an adventure with the family. Get off the beaten path with a friend. Blaze a new trail.

Successful kids explore the world of possibilities.

SUCCESS TIP # 100
EXPERIMENT

Check it out. Test it and see. It's trial and error. Run an experiment. Try it out. You won't know until you try. What are you waiting for? Go ahead, EXPERIMENT!

Successful kids take risks and experiment with new things. Just remember all the tips in the section on safety.

Take SAFE RISKS when you experiment with new things.

SUCCESS TIP # 101
TAKE OFF THE TRAINING WHEELS

Just about everyone who has learned to ride a bike started out using training wheels. It was one way to ride a "big boy" or "big girl" bike when you didn't have the balancing idea figured out yet. But there came a time when you had to take a risk and remove the training wheels and learn to ride without them.

There comes a time in life when you have to take the risk and do things that are hard at first. You have to risk reading a book at a higher level. You have to risk trying multiplication or algebra. You have to risk speaking in front of others.

As we grow up, we will be confronted with many opportunities to try new things, take risks, and learn from our mistakes. But if you never take off the training wheels, you may never learn anything new.

CONCLUSION

We've pretty much given you everything we have learned about being a successful kid and living a responsible life. In fact, you could say that we've shown you how our mom and dad parent, how our Bondy and grandma live their life, how our dad's best friend interacts with us, how our grandma plays and how our uncle and aunt take care of family. These success tips are just the way we all try to live in our family.

We have lots of growing up ahead of us and way more to learn. But we think we have a good start with these success tips. Who knows, in the next of couple years we might have more tips to share. For now, we're going to use these tips as best we can.

What about you? Are you ready to pick a few of the tips and start living them? The only way you're going to become who you want to be as a kid is to take action. Don't wait to be a grown-up. Be who you want to be now. Take action now. Be successful now. Use our success tips now.

Reese Haller

Photo by Mark Bradford

Reese is eleven years old and in seventh grade. He is considered one of the youngest published fiction authors in America. Reese is the author of the award-winning *Fred the Mouse*™ series, which includes four chapter books for readers in the second through fourth grades. Visit www.fredthemouse.com for more information.

Reese began writing short stories in kindergarten, where he was encouraged to take risks with his writing. He discovered his joy and passion in the third grade, where he blossomed as a writer.

Reese has been a regular presenter at elementary schools across the country since 2005, where he lectures on how to inspire children to write in a captivating 60-minute presentation. He has presented live to over 15,000 people in teacher in-services, keynote addresses, and numerous elementary classrooms discussing writing and publishing. In October 2007 Reese was the keynote speaker at Central Michigan University for their Make a Difference Day. Reese has also appeared live on *The Martha Stewart Show,* reaching thousands with his message about writing and reading.

Reese has been appointed the Ambassador of Literacy for the Youth of Michigan by Michigan's Governor, Jennifer Granholm. He has also been appointed to the National Advisory Council for the Statue of Responsibility, a United States National monument to be unveiled in July of 2010. He is a featured author, along with Oprah, Stephen Covey, Barack Obama, Pope John Paul, George S. McGovern, and 55 other authors, in a book entitled *Responsibility 911*, published in support of the national monument. He is the only child featured in this book.

For more information, visit Reese at www.reesehaller.com

Parker Haller

Parker is eight years old and in the third grade. He has been writing books since the age of four. Parker published his first book at the age of seven, a series of mini-books about animals for preschool and kindergarten children. It includes over 140 pencil drawings of animals drawn by the author himself.

Parker is completing his third book, a chapter book for first-graders entitled *Piggy Goes to Space*. Its release date is scheduled for March of 2009. Just in time for National Reading Month.

Parker is also the editor-in-chief of a monthly newspaper called *The Haller Gazette*. He initiated the idea of a newspaper by kids for kids as a fun summer writing and reading activity in the spring of 2008. As the editor-in-chief, Parker makes all the editorial decisions for *The Haller Gazette*, which currently reaches children in twenty-eight states. To sign up for your copy, simply e-mail your name and postal address to parker@thomashaller.com.

To learn more about what Parker is getting into next, visit his website at www.parkerhaller.com.

Other books by Reese and Parker

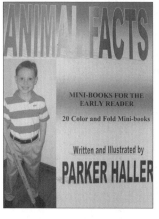

ANIMAL FACTS: Mini-Books for the Early Reader
Written and Illustrated by Parker Haller

MINI-BOOKS FOR THE EARLY READER

20 Color and Fold Mini-books

Written and Illustrated by

PARKER HALLER

Paperback book ($9.95) - Available through Personal Power Press, Inc. www.personalpowerpress.com - 877.360.1477

Children are moved and inspired to read with this collection of twenty mini-books written and illustrated by seven-year-old Parker Haller. Each mini-book is eight pages in length, with one animal fact sentence and a picture to color on each page. This mini-book collection includes over 140 hand-drawn illustrations. Simply remove each mini-book from the main booklet and fold into a 2 x 4-inch book perfect for young readers.

FRED THE MOUSE™ BOOK SERIES
By Reese Haller

Fred the Mouse™ Book One: The Adventures Begin
by Reese Haller

The *Fred the Mouse™* book series is written by 8-year-old author Reese Haller - www.personalpowerpress.com/aboutReese.html.

Learn how Fred uses his intuition and trusts his inner-knowing to stay out of trouble. This delightful book can be shared as a read-aloud with young children and as an independent reading book for 2nd - 4th graders. *Fred the Mouse™: The Adventures Begin* is a Benjamin Franklin Award silver medal winner.

Fred the Mouse™
Book Two: Making Friends
by Reese Haller
The second book in the Fred the Mouse™ book series by 9-year-old author Reese Haller. - www.personalpowerpress.com/aboutReese.html

The adventures continue as Fred befriends a snake, barn swallow, crow, turtle, cat and watchdog. A powerful story of the acceptance of diversity and uniqueness that even young children can understand. *Fred the Mouse™: Making Friends* is a Mom's Choice Awards Gold Medal winner.

Fred the Mouse™
Book Three: Rescuing Freedom
by Reese Haller
The third book in the Fred the Mouse™ book series by 9-year-old author Reese Haller. - www.personalpowerpress.com/aboutReese.html

The magnificent adventures of Fred lead him to discover the meaning of freedom. Children will be moved by the insightful message about the concept of freedom woven into the delightful story. *Fred the Mouse™: Rescuing Freedom* was nominated for a Newbery Award.

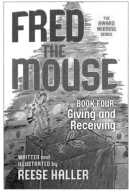

Fred the Mouse™
Book Four: Giving and Receiving
by Reese Haller
The fourth book in the Fred the Mouse™ book series by 10-year-old author Reese Haller. - www.personalpowerpress.com/aboutReese.html

Book Four masterfully blends another adventure of Fred the Mouse with an extraordinary message of being a generous giver as well as a gracious receiver.